CHARLOTTE RAMPLING

with Christophe Bataille

translated from the French by William Hobson
with Charlotte Rampling

WHO I AM

ICON

Published in the UK
in 2017
by Icon Books Ltd,
Omnibus Business Centre,
39–41 North Road,
London N7 9DP
email: info@iconbooks.com
www.iconbooks.com

Sold in the UK,
Europe and Asia
by Faber & Faber Ltd,
Bloomsbury House,
74–77 Great Russell Street,
London WC1B 3DA
or their agents

Distributed in the UK,
Europe and Asia
by Grantham Book Services,
Trent Road,
Grantham
NG31 7XQ

Distributed in Australia and
New Zealand
by Allen & Unwin Pty Ltd,
PO Box 8500, 83 Alexander Street,
Crows Nest, NSW 2065

Distributed in South Africa
by Jonathan Ball, Office B4,
The District, 41 Sir Lowry Road,
Woodstock 7925

Distributed in India
by Penguin Books India,
7th Floor, Infinity Tower – C,
DLF Cyber City,
Gurgaon 122002, Haryana

Distributed in Canada
by Publishers Group Canada,
76 Stafford Street, Unit 300,
Toronto, Ontario M6J 2S1

Distributed in the USA
by Publishers Group West,
1700 Fourth Street,
Berkeley, CA 94710

ISBN: 978-1-78578-193-3

Typeset in Granjon by Marie Doherty

Printed and bound in the UK
by Clays Ltd, St Ives plc

For Barnaby, Émilie, David.

Today, Charlotte, you seem worried and you say with a laugh, 'I don't know what this book *is* anymore ... What did we say, that it would be my childhood or a sort of portrait, I've lost track. One thing it definitely can't be is a biography. I've tried telling my life story, it doesn't work.

And it would be good if I actually liked the book we make together. Is that possible? To genuinely accept it, like it? I recoil from definitions, narrations, you know that, Christophe. I don't open up.'

Who I Am: not a biography, or a song, or a betrayal, barely a novel — let's say a ballad, one of those ones you hum, like *The Ballad of the Ladies of Times Past*. You are one of those ladies whatever era you come from: I see you in photographs, haughty, often naked in your twenties, in a short skirt, black stockings, playful, in your own world. With that effortlessly elusive smile.

You make your gaze clear-eyed. *Dive into me*: you'll never see what I see.

Everything is true in our book. Or rather: everything has happened. Dialogue, images, memories. Occasionally I've changed the clothes people were wearing. I've added some colour to the silence, and some words – just a few.

It all starts at an editorial meeting. A typical Wednesday: we are dreaming aloud in the office where Radiguet signed the contract for *The Devil in the Flesh*. Parquet floor, classical mouldings, wallpaper sky. Dreaming is the word for it. There is something unreal about great books.

On this particular Wednesday one of us brings up your name; he met you at a dinner. You are difficult. Dangerous. Bristling with *lawyers*. The word cruises between us like a shark. But who isn't difficult? An editor announces that your official biography has been taken on by a talented, formidable female American journalist and already sold to a French publisher. For a fortune. We drop the subject.

I ask a friend for your address. He shrugs genially and I dash off a letter to you that same evening. The challenge, the game. Your defiant solitude. To *be* you. To understand. To find the right words.

You were sweet, really, the first time we met, Charlotte; years ago now. Of course this expression makes you bristle. 'Sweetness, no … Christophe, don't overdo it … It's only the third page! Why not throw in my kindness, my even temper while we're at it?'

I can feel your reticence. Your wary shyness. How familiar all this is to you. How tired you are of being stared at, desired. Imagined. And second-guessed. What better way could there be of not listening to you? It is as if there is someone imprisoned in your legendary name.

Men come and see me in the night. Men watch me and steal my secrets. I leave a fleeting image, fragments of feeling, sensations … I watch the men, I see them in the half-light, I listen to their breathing. The screen separates us. And who knows … who knows what is transformed by these images.

I am waiting for you, I feel a little afraid – of your intelligence, of your challenging gaze, of your fear. Here you are. Long beige coat. We order quickly and quietly.

You break into a smile. Your 'celebrity memoirs' will never be published. The moment you saw the first chapters, you put a stop to it. All those details, those anecdotes, those empty words. You give me the names of publishers and agents in Paris and New York, as if I needed proof. No book will be done without Charlotte Rampling and no book will be done with her. Wanting everything, forbidding everything.

So does that mean I have to obey? Keep my distance? Be a wallflower?

I look at your delicate, fine-skinned hands, which seem to be searching for something. Time has passed through those fingers, desire, playfulness, wisdom, I don't know, children's laughter.

When it's my turn, I say my piece: 'I haven't come here with advances or contracts. I just want to give it a go. Head towards childhood. And if you call this off too, if you swallow the key to the safe, so be it. The pages will remain. That's the way it is with books you dream of.'

Now you finish my glass of burgundy. 'You don't mind? It's a good way to begin, don't you think?' Yes, Charlotte, it's a good beginning. Then you laugh.

You've given me writings from different periods of your life, contemplative paragraphs, meditative thoughts. I've tried to be you, Charlotte. To know you a little. Never to hurt you. I thought that, come what may, your name would be on this book. That you would be the sole source of whatever is in it. That it would be a portrait and a self-portrait. A pact, that was what I said.

My name is Tessa Rampling. Charlotte is my middle name, but it took over. Tessa became Charlotte.

Ever since I was born, I have been haunted by this feeling of what comes into your life and is then gone, what wounds you, what you can't control. Children imagine things, they make up stories.

The laughter and the tears become indistinguishable. We lock them away. For the Ramplings, the heart is a safe. Kept by generations, the family secret becomes a legend. We only know how to keep silent.

People stare at you. They come closer. They back away.

No hint of trembling as you stand naked in the galleries of the Louvre where La Tour and Fra Filippo Lippi dream. The Mona Lisa is looking at you through her bulletproof glass case. There's no half-light here. Everything is hidden by the dazzling light of the photographer. Now you break into a smile: where are the museum attendants, the works of art, the silk dresses, the togas and jewels, the symbols, the crucifixes and headdresses? Where is the history of art, in all its infinite seriousness …?

The Madonna, *c'est moi*.

Come and get me if you can.

I show up at your address, ring the bell and wait. A few doors down there's a shop that makes knives. A Chinese chemist. An antiquarian book dealer. I daydream as I wait.

Then you appear, black trousers, worn trench coat: So Christophe, are you lost? Are you looking for me out here, on the street?

Spring has come. We've arranged to meet in the Luxembourg Gardens. We walk through the park in silence. I look at your sandals, which are dusty, like a child's. There is a little stain on your trousers. We end up sitting at a metal table. Bad coffee. A girl signals wildly – Is it her? Is it her? – she asks you for an autograph. You give her a sweet smile. She can't believe it.

'It's fine, really …' you whisper. I walk you back to your front door two hours and three sentences later. Shattered portrait.

I look in the mirror and see a woman I do not recognise. A mosaic face made up of random pieces chosen by chance. A collection of expressions chosen and rearranged to form a face.

It must be hard being Charlotte Rampling. Talking is hard. Writing is hard. The words don't come.

So you have to meet a writer, a mild-mannered vampire, a tenacious creature with four hands and two heads. Don't invent. Don't steal. Talk a little. Listen. Then take that part of you that doesn't open up.

Your secret apartment. It's so you, I think: the white rooms, the sloping parquet floor, the bound novels of Thomas Mann and Charlotte Brontë above the fireplace.

I ring the bell. Here you are. Shoulder-
length hair. Bare feet. Shy smile. Clear gaze.
'Hello, come in …' you hold out a hand stiffly,
like all English women who don't kiss hello.

We go through the shadowy hall; to my
right, I make out a kitchen. An abandoned
cup. On the left, a sideboard, a few art books,
a painting. I feel like a thief in an empty house.
But I haven't stolen anything yet, no photos or
notebooks, no pieces of your soul.

Your office in the attic. A divan covered
with a rough woven fabric. Wordlessly you
point me to a chair ten feet away.

We talk and laugh in French, occasionally
in English.

Off to one side, a stained drafting table.
Some soft brushes. A few tubes of paint.
Everything is immaculate. Give the walls your
paintings that bear the mark of your knife.

When it's time to leave, I say:

'I like this adventure. Like a secret.'

We choose a date. Next time I'll take notes. You smile:

'You know, Christophe, I like disappearing. That's how it is. I see people for a while, then I don't see them. Maybe we'll never see each other again.'

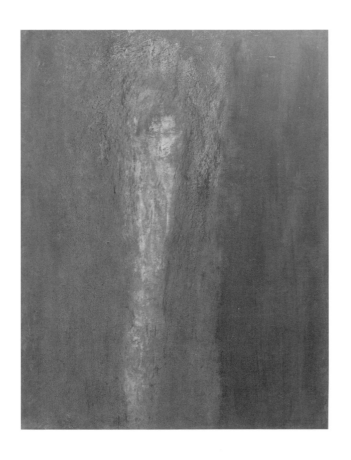

I think of your paintings: always the same graceful, anxious silhouette caught in black gouache. How many times have I wanted to take one of them with me as I was leaving? But I'm not as brave as you: I didn't do it.

I can wait. I have the time and I have the choice,
I am even spoiled for choice.
Only chance can heed the call of my choice.
When it comes, by chance, it's the absolute proof of my choice.

One day, it's not the day. The door is open on the fifth floor. I cross the long living room. Sitting on the edge of the divan, legs splayed like a boy, you hold a record in your hand. We dive deep into words, guitars, dreams. I don't say much. In front of us, the *hi-fi*, as it used to be, the old material world in black and yellow casing with its heavy remote control. The era of cassette tapes is not far off.

We listen to a song in silence, then two, then five. You bow your head, clasping your hands. I feel weak, my muscles ache. When the music ends, you say, 'Well, Christophe, when shall we see each other again?'

The family safe was sealed forever by Godfrey, your father, who won gold at the Berlin Olympics in 1936. As for me, my role is clear. I'll write, narrate, interpret, but as you know, Charlotte, the Knight never sets the Maiden free.

You've always written, like your mother. When she was fifteen she recorded her daily activities in purple ink in a pretty notebook. Today – but what is this never-ending today? – you want a book to exist and you want it to be your heart.

I stare into your grey eyes: only part of you is there. You are looking beyond me.

This is how secrets are made. Place yourself at the centre of the world and stare at us from behind those eyes.

You want to escape the history of film, which tells its own story anyway. You want childhood. The poetry of childhood. From our first meeting those words came to me.

I walk forwards, I walk backwards, one step behind the other. I walk backwards towards myself. Endlessly returning to the point of departure. The start of the beginning. The beginning of my life. Who I am.

I was born in my maternal grandparents' home and spent the first months of my life there. A big Victorian manor house all brick and greenery, near Cambridge. They had given it a strangely romantic name: 'Coupals'. The war was ending. My father came home on leave from Malta, kissed me and within a day had returned to the island, scanning the sea and the sand. The history of men.

I can see my mother approaching, radiant, in almond green tulle and taffeta, her makeup glowing. She loves fairy tales, kings and queens, dresses with trains, crystal tears. The feeling that all is good in the world.

She is dressed for a ball. Is she always this elegant?

It's the early 1950s. My mother takes me in her arms, kisses me briefly as if there is no time, no lasting happiness, no promises for the girl who clings to her dress, searching for a way to be loved. And then she disappears into the night.

When you have a secret, you cherish it. You hold it close. The secret grows, never fades. Sometimes it slips out, a word, a look. And it becomes a memory.

I like looking at little girls. I listen to them, I look at their tangled hair, their innocent hands: I see my secret in their eyes.

My mother is the heroine of a romantic novel. Her carefree youth is mirrored in the happy pages of *The Great Gatsby*.

It's spring and the party of the season is about to begin. Everything is satin and perfumed silk. A photographer catches the moment. Fitzgerald wasn't dreaming. This side of Paradise is all too real. That long car drawn up beside the steps of an elegant mansion is not some relic from a distant past: it is my mother's youth.

Alongside her sister, three years older, my mother lived the glamorous heyday of the 1920s. Both were pretty and pampered, young debutantes whose affections every eligible bachelor in Cambridge dreamed of winning at the ball. Before the carriages came and carried off their grace and delight and my childhood dreams ...

My mother loved to laugh, to dance, to play. She was entrancing. She let life carry her along. She was a butterfly by day and a princess by night.

She was at the glittering heart of the social whirl. Naturally she never worked. There was no question or need of such a thing.

The Gurteens were not aristocrats but they were a prominent family. Highly respected weavers by trade, they still have their factories at Haverhill two centuries later. They started off making religious vestments, then moved on to army uniforms, and ended up dressing the whole town. Today, my cousin Christopher manages the factory, which is listed as a site of historical significance. Modern machinery has been installed in its workshops of glass and steel.

One day my mother's brother William invites one of his friends home. They are both twenty. In a startling *coup de foudre*, my mother realises that the man standing there, a stiff figure in his military uniform, will be the love of her life. She is just twelve. The handsome athlete, a saturnine, distant young man, ill at ease with the world, is already training for the Olympics.

Godfrey Lionel Rampling's entrance into her life is feverishly recorded by Isabel Ann Gurteen in her journal in flowery ink.

My father was six when his father was killed in battle in Basra, then under British mandate. It was 1915. Between heaven and hell. Between the Tigris and the Euphrates. His mother Gertrude was left a widow with three children. She was penniless but brave and tenacious. She remarried fairly quickly, but her new husband didn't want to take on three children.

So they decided to keep the two youngest, Barbara and Kenneth. My father was sent to his maternal grandmother in her Victorian manor in the countryside. A radical, devastating separation. A reasoned act of abandonment. That's how it was back then and you didn't argue.

My great-grandmother was a severe woman. My father found himself not only orphaned but sent to boarding school. He was only seven.

Such, therefore, was the lonely childhood of the great Godfrey Rampling, colonel in the Royal Artillery. How many times did he see his family? He never said. He was impenetrable. And I never dared ask.

I love this child who will emerge victorious, always angling for a smile, the slightest sign of affection. He is reaching for the sky where he can forget the world and start all over.

I love this man who keeps the world at a distance: never give anything to those who betray you.

Little, so little, so wild that I am.
Silent witness of out of control gestures.
I use silence as a voice without using words.
And wait for the spring to awake me.

What is the world? A bed on four legs.

What is a hero? A child on an island of cotton and sheets.

What is a man? A child who closes his eyes and sees his past.

And you, the crowd cheers you on, gold glints in your hand and you take refuge in the glory that maybe forgets but never forgives.

The trees envelop us, arching low and green over the avenues of the park. You speak in a whisper. I think I hear you say you're just back from several months in California, where you've been playing the part of a psychiatrist.

Under your arm, a big photograph album from your childhood: a stout, yellowing volume annotated by your mother. It had been in storage in South London, in an iron trunk. A street in Fontainebleau. Dunes where two little girls are playing. Forgotten images. Handwritten captions.

You see, Christophe, people say you have to create a mystique. So I hid away here.

In a pastel profusion of satin and lace I fall onto a soft bed and disappear into a velvet world of sensation. Coloured silks moulding the bodies of her princesses, my mother relishes her daughters' transformation with every fibre of her being.

Her scarlet mouth kisses the colours, her hands run sensually over the materials. Ecstasy every time the party begins. Peals of delighted laughter. Two picture perfect little girls.

Is it going to go on like this, my life as a river, the river of my life? What am I meant to do? The contrasts are so strong. I can't see my face anymore.

But Charlotte: storytelling is a wonderful thing and this is not play-acting.

One day my mother can no longer leave her room. My father dresses her, feeds her, listens to her. Pushes her wheelchair. He plays her husband and her whole world. He becomes the guardian of her life.

The years go by. The notebooks in purple ink fade away. Growing old is difficult. She is like a small bird on a branch, gently swinging, sweetly smiling.

Sitting at her bedside, my father and I finally talk. I think of my sister Sarah, whose beautiful face still seems close enough to touch.

My father, who had never written a diary or a memoir, who had always kept his joys, sorrows and thoughts to himself, didn't want to die before his wife. He didn't want there to be a chance she could be left on her own.

While preparing to move to their last home, he did a strange thing: he took his wife's writings and the diaries she had kept since she was twelve, along with all her photos and hundreds of letters, stuffed them into big plastic bags and … put them all out on the pavement, without saying anything to anyone.

You laughed as you told me this, Charlotte, and I felt your sadness. Freud loved the story of Gradiva, who walks through sun-scorched Pompeii in a white toga: alive, dead, a figure from a dream, she wakes us from our sleep. We should find an equivalent deity for your father, Charlotte. A name for this enigma: this young man who runs in the stadiums, powerful, winged. The sun transforming everything.

But did you love him?

You look down. It is neither a yes nor a no. Silence falls, overwhelms you.

Then you look at me for a long time before you break into a smile. This is to be your answer. I feel as if I already knew it. The secret is not in melancholy, but maybe in its vital essence, in its silent beauty that never ceases to intrigue and remains still at the heart of everything.

Through the window I look out at the trees etched against the sky. Skeletal forms waiting for the transformation to begin. They lend themselves to the cycle of life that man, in his uncertainty, refuses. I close my eyes before nature's truth. I wait for words to come. Inspiration glides in on a breath.

A little man in a hat rings the bell of my house in London. I open the door to a character straight out of Dickens. He quickly explains that he is in possession of certain items that might be of interest to me.

I wrote that the heart is a safe, but no, the heart is a bag. To prove he is serious, he takes a sample from his satchel, 'but I have much more': a twelve-year-old girl's exercise book, photos of my mother in evening dress, a certificate for good behaviour, newspaper articles, letters. A life snatched from the dump.

I ring my father. Why have some London dealers got their hands on our family treasures? I want to know. I insist. I beg him. But he doesn't answer, he refuses to say anything until suddenly, in a violent voice, he shouts, 'I THREW THEM AWAY!'

I'm devastated. I picture the overflowing bin bags being carted off by the rubbish van, impacted and stacked in piles before disappearing forever into the flames. But there is a god of thieves.

The little man in the hat started talking money. His friends were asking for an insane amount. He claimed vaguely to be a collector, a dealer. He specialised in things connected to the Olympics, certificates, photos, documents. I imagined him at his stall in the East End hawking stolen medals, guns and trinkets.

We did the deal, he counted the money twice and we shook hands.

And that was how I bought back my mother's youth.

After the war, my father was broke. He tried to sell his gold medal or have it melted down. He went to a jeweller's in London and discovered it was made of steel. Hitler had tricked the athletes, palmed them off with fakes. The medal simply disappeared after that, possibly lost in one of our moves.

It mattered and it didn't matter to my father, who was engaged in a desperate quest which took him far beyond.

I sealed the boxes away in an iron trunk. All that life, virtually within reach. I never reopened it.

A young girl in a crêpe dress is sitting on the backboard of a caravan. She is barefoot in this paradise of graceful black and white flowers. Some sort of poison hangs in the air, I don't know what it is. Was she thinking of something when the photograph was taken? She looks at me so sweetly.

I was ready to ride away into my dream of woods and wind, the daughter of melancholy and laughter, but in the end I stayed.

Well, this photo without an album is for you, Christophe. For you who were looking for a legend and found a child.

I wish I could touch Tessa Charlotte Rampling's beautiful face as she waits on the threshold of adulthood. I would like to tell you not to worry, that it will often be difficult and opaque, inhuman even, but you will give us so much – all of us – and this book will be part of it.

I listen to a director discussing his film. He laughs mirthlessly, dread is in the air, in his films, in his strange, muffled voice. Suddenly he says my name followed by these words: 'a sense of ghost'.

Yes, Charlotte, that's it: a sense of ghost, appearing and disappearing, talking to the living, cherishing the departed, searching for your name, your face as you glide light-footed through cinema and literature. I see your hand on the page and screen, slender and pure, pushing it away and grabbing hold of life.

One day, I found you seemingly lost in front of a cardboard box you had wheeled over on a metal trolley from the Boulevard Saint Michel. Your hair was tousled and you were smiling. I thought of Gena Rowlands. Of Barbara Loden in *Wanda*. I didn't say anything.

I didn't know you at seven in a pleated skirt and white blouse in Norfolk; I never came across you in a miniskirt in Chelsea in the sixties, but isn't it better like this?

I opened the box, unpacked the machine, attached the nozzle, plugged it in and set about vacuuming your apartment with meticulous care. You followed me around, laughing. When I finished, you whispered: 'I've been in this place twenty years, and I've never vacuumed. You had to appear.'

With this remark worthy of Miss Havisham in her palace of dust, we sat down to talk.

One mustn't of course become attached. I must forget your phone number, your two home addresses, your email address. I must write without expecting an answer. Believe that silence always wins. Remember that it's not a scheme or a strategy. Keep heading towards the child you once were.

Swaffham in Norfolk, once a small town. The trains go no further, it's the end of the line – but country roads push on beyond. Past the rose-entwined gorse hedges that shelter the fields, the long beaches stretch out empty and windswept towards the sea. Brancaster Beach. I walk past The Greyhound Inn and I see the huge granite church and, further on, the colonnaded bandstand with a goddess adorning its dome. It is 1950.

My father has been posted here for two years and I don't know how to put it exactly, but something is wrong. We are living in a plain, neat little house, furnished with the few bits and pieces that follow us around from place to place. Army life, regimented down to the last detail. Discipline is paramount.

Rather than a 'sense of ghost' there's a 'sense of unease'. It's a gentle sort of haunting.

Sarah is sent to boarding school miles away because there isn't a good school nearby. I feel like I'm losing my sister, my only friend.

And you, mother, you who would sing us those nursery rhymes that I remember still, you who were always so tender and light, how did you cope?

Childhood is a mystery.

I was seven and something happened at school. I remember a disgusting meal. I remember my plate. I remember the checked tablecloth. My hands clenching. My fury. Suddenly I'm getting up. I'm fleeing the dining hall, fleeing the school, running as if wolves are at my heels, running as fast as my father, running for my life.

I get to the house and then I don't remember what happened. All I know is that I was sent almost immediately to the same boarding school as Sarah. And our parents were left on their own in the little house in Swaffham.

My country is heavy as lead. It drags me down into melancholy. It leaves me with a sense of unease. I look at the neat little houses like soldiers in perfectly straight lines. The lawns perfectly mown. The dogs perfectly trained to avoid disturbing the neighbour. The neighbour so sorry for disturbing the dog. Behind the net curtains I imagine a quiet life. But my unease tells me a different story.

It's early May now and I read what we've written. You're still here. It's strange. You haven't run away, nor have I.

If this is a poem, Christophe, if we end up knowing so few things, if everything is genuinely laid bare, then don't be angry with me. I'll add a word, a comma, a breath, and I'll disappear into the wind.

For as long as I can remember, there were worries about Sarah. When we were reunited at boarding school, she was my ten-year-old sister.

She used to get up at night and sleepwalk, along the corridors, haunted by dreams. Our instructions were clear: do not wake her!

She would take her blanket and a pillow with her. We would find her in the early hours snuggled up in someone else's bed, my big and little sister. It was a dangerous tale: where were we going to find Sarah tomorrow?

My sister spent hours in front of the mirror trying to understand. She challenged a forbidden taboo and found death before she could find the answer. Mirrors have since been forbidden. The appearance of things must remain an enigma.

Sarah was like a beautiful doll: pale por-
celain skin, big eyes looking into the future,
blonde hair that Mum was constantly combing
and smoothing. Sarah was pampered, preened,
kissed … She needed looking after. I have this
memory of beauty overshadowed by exhaus-
tion, unease and these words: 'Charlotte, take
care of your sister.' My big and little sister:
'look after her.' The classic English novel with
a pale child coughing in her bedroom. When
she was about five, Sarah was operated on, but
she remained fragile all her life, like a flower
that is not truly meant for this world.

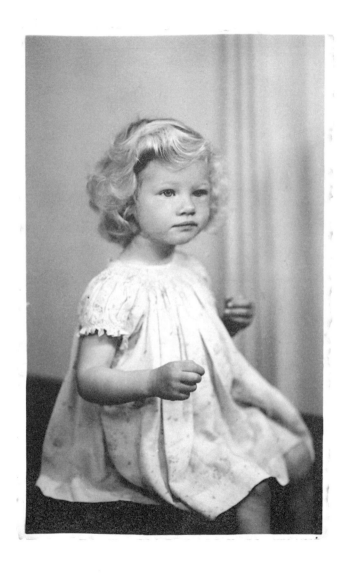

When he returned from Malta in 1946, my father was posted here and there to different points of the compass. Those were the days when Her Majesty's Kingdom, like France and America, covered vast expanses of territory.

We moved seven times in thirteen years. Wherever we went, I knew that each new friend would soon be lost. I knew that one day my father would announce, 'We're leaving. I've been posted to Gibraltar. Or Wales. Or Norfolk.' And once again we'd pack up our school books and favourite toys, put our furniture into store, fold our clothes, kiss the old times goodbye and not look back. Living like that, Sarah was my one great friend.

It ended up becoming a part of me, like a discipline or a torment: I knew I was going to leave and that I wouldn't come back.

*I stand up straight like the lieutenant my
father would have me be. I submit to orders that
make no sense. I carry out duties without knowing what they are. I obey to be loved for the child
that I am.*

*I wear the doll's dresses that my mother makes.
I sleep in curlers to have hair like hers. I smile to
be loved for the child that I am.*

You're not easy to describe, Sarah. I circle
around you. Around us. Around our childhood, our games, our dancing, our moving
homes. Around your beautiful face. Your life
eludes me. You elude me.

You were nearly three when I was born.
We were still living at our grandparents'
house. I was handed over to a nanny almost
immediately because Mum was worried about
you. She was afraid and wanted to be by your
side every minute of the day.

Afterwards my mother told me that she regretted not having been able to be there for me. It's true, I've always had the feeling of being kept at a distance. And you, Sarah? You didn't get to know our father until you were three.

Childhood is its own small battleground.

We watch a soldier in uniform come through the door. His face gaunt from so many horrors. Our father has come home. He looks at us but he doesn't see us. He talks to us but can't find the right words. Tired of his inadequacy, he retreats into silence.

When he was very young my father had set his heart on joining the Royal Air Force. He dreamt of becoming a young god flying close to the sun, seeking glory above the clouds.

Godfrey Lionel Rampling was tall and strong, and he breezed through the RAF College's exams. But he suffered from nerves, and when he had to take a simple breathing test, he flunked it.

Devastated, my father had no choice but to join the artillery. He was earthbound, permanently grounded.

This setback propelled him on. Physical weakness was transformed into a rage to win. He found within himself the breath the doctors had refused. He ran like the wind, in a state of grace. The arena at Olympia rose to applaud him. He was no longer a man but an angel, a winged demigod fallen to earth. He was Ariel. But England is not Crete, and our labyrinths are gardens.

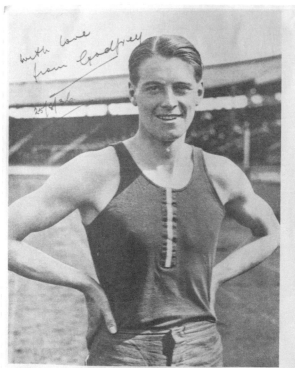

G. RAMPLING, THE OUTSTANDING PERFORMER
IN BRITAIN'S RELAY VICTORY

ly running his 400 metre leg of the 1,600 metre relay in a little over 46 seconds and retrieving lost ground Rampling was argely instrumental in this event being won for Great Britain. It was our only track running success in the Olympic Games

The world reveres his masterful skills but he invents illnesses as a way of avoiding them.

The force that launched him onto the paths of glory turns against him and wreaks havoc.

I know very little about the Ramplings. About my father's grandmother, who took him when he was seven. About his father, who died in Basra. About his stepfather who gave him away. No one talked. It was a time when you didn't ask questions. Later, when I began to ask people about the family, no one seemed to remember. It was as if nothing had happened, no farewells, no smiles, no sorrows, no songs. And yet the images keep flowing past, soft or hard-edged, jostling me, and I end up loving them – and the people they depict – more than the spoken word.

I love what I read.

Everything ends up surprising me.

I am ready for the world of language and words.

Two brothers look at one another. Their eyes take in the same image. Discomfort flickers back and forth, transmitted by their gaze.

They look down, embarrassed by their discomfort.

The Royal Air Force demands the ultimate sacrifice of a blind courage that knows no limits. The Royal Air Force, in all its majesty, takes the brother who is prepared to give his life in this way. The ultimate sacrifice of a glorious death consigns my father to the shadows.

Group Captain Kenneth Johnson Rampling was shot down over Frankfurt in his Lancaster in 1944.

Away we go to the sea
To have a jolly good spree,
We'll dig and run and have a jolly good tea,
We'll have eggs and ham and lots of
strawberry jam
And then we'll have a lettuce too
And then we'll think of something to do.
Away we go to the sea
To have a jolly good spree.

I remember us singing and laughing. The eggs would get all mixed up with the strawberry jam and the ham. My father would join in, in a voice more used to booming God Save the Queen. Our little car would rock from side to side and I'd imagine it was our nursery, or a horse drawn carriage, or a Lancaster bomber plunging towards the dunes that stretched out before the sea.

When we arrived at Fontainebleau in France, everything seemed exotic: the school, the clothes, the food, the houses, the colours.

We lived on a quiet street at the edge of the forest. A house of grey stone in the midst of incredible trees. My room was in a small, pink tower. Sarah's looked onto the garden. We spent hours in the forest with our dog Tinka. It was pure freedom. Everything was changing. It was the beginning of our revolution.

My father's batman would come every morning to attend to him, and then he would set off to the Allied Forces' headquarters. This was a whole world unto itself, with its school, shops, swimming pool, social life. It seems remote today that world, half black-and-white, half colour, encapsulated in the phrase: the postwar years.

My parents were nonconformists, in their own way. Even though we were Protestant, they enrolled us in a Catholic school, le Collège Jeanne d'Arc. We didn't understand a thing. Not a word. Quite apart from the decimal system, which was a complete mystery to us with our pounds, shillings and pence.

No one spoke English. My father would listen to records every morning as he shaved, repeating endlessly, *'Bonjour Paul, comment allez-vous? Paul, as-tu garé la voiture?'*

And this mysterious Paul would never deign to reply.

In the summer we would go down south to La Croix-Valmer. A retired English colonel ran a very beautiful campsite overlooking the sea.

My parents trust us and leave us free to do what we want because we respect their rules. We spend wonderful days with boys and girls of our age in the shade of the pine trees or on the beach, caught up in a sunlit dream. At night we lie by the fire, sing songs, talk in whispers. Such happiness feels as if it will never end.

Sarah is fourteen and I watch her smile subtly change, that opaque, slightly distracted smile of hers. The innocence, the not knowing, how do we recapture that? What name shall we give it? All childhood is bathed in light.

There should be a list of happy days. To preserve them, cherish them, and then of course not believe them. How many diaries does one need not to remember?

I'm coming, Sarah. I want to tell our story. I want to be with you.

When you turned twenty-one, our parents gave you your first big trip abroad. With a girl-friend, you left London for America. You went to New York and then your tour of the continent took you to Acapulco, that spectacular strip of land pinned between the ocean and the mountains.

This is where you met Carlos. A handsome, older man. A rich Argentinian cattle rancher, a man of experience. And there you did something very strange, Sarah. Without saying anything to anyone, a week after meeting him, you married him.

I read about it in a newspaper in London.
My mother was frantic. She couldn't bear the
thought of Sarah being so far away.

Sarah would come back with Carlos from
time to time. Gradually we sensed that this
separation from her language, her country,
her culture, her family, was starting to weigh
on her.

Three years after they married, my mother is at her sewing machine. Her body suddenly gives way. She goes completely limp and slumps forward onto the table.

She pulls herself together as best she can and manages to drive to the nearby golf course where my father is working.

A few hours later, the phone rings at home: at the very moment my mother had collapsed, Sarah had died in Argentina.

The voice of suffering is an innocent voice. It leaves no room for certainties. It leaves no room for vanity. It leaves no room for others.

I was making a film for television at the time. I was playing a young woman from the 1900s, a spirited girl throwing off the shackles of convention. She embodied the sense of life coursing through me.

When I get to my parents' house, I see my father push open the little garden gate and come towards me. He announces in a loud voice: 'Your sister is dead.' That was how I found out. 'Go and see your mother.' Which I did, leaving him lost and alone in the middle of the garden.

My mother is in an armchair in the living room. I kneel in front of her. She takes my hand and holds onto me as if she will never let me go, as if she is going to take me with her. I struggle and gently try to pull away. She holds fast, she is hurting me. Suddenly she releases her grip and falls into unconsciousness.

For many years afterwards she is inconsolable. With Sarah, everything went out of her life.

A stubborn refusal to be tamed. A relentless quest. A primal solitude. An unyielding struggle.

Absurd sometimes. Excessive. Wilful. Since forever inflamed.

For the Ramplings, there was no body, no funeral. Sarah had disappeared. When the phone rang that evening, she had already been buried. Because of the heat, we were told.

All I know is that Sarah has lain in her husband's family vault since February 1967.

For some reason I still cannot explain, I have never been to Argentina.

My memory leaves me with an impression. An outline without detail, a fragment without form. The image fades leaving a reminiscence of absence. A disturbing sense of being out of time. It's just an impression, but the impression remains.

Tell me, Charlotte, what have we been doing in this book all these years?

Until my twenties I used to be called Charley. By my parents, my friends, my sister. I was Charley.

Sometimes, you just have to reach out your hand: mine rests on a nineteen-year-old girl's. Bent over her desk, Charley is sticking articles and photographs into a scrapbook, conscientiously captioning them.

There I am, in a tweed dress, below-the-knee or very short. There I am, lying on the boot of a car, or hidden by flowers, or standing next to my father in a double-breasted suit, or with a group of actors. I'm laughing, humming a tune. A man is stroking my hair or putting his arm around my waist.

There's Sarah too, in a 'New Look' dress and silk gloves, looking hesitant at an award ceremony.

Sarah and her photographer friend, Roland. Sarah, so happy.

I close the photo album. I'll leave you now, Charley, it seems as if my name left with Sarah.

And I can never again hold a young girl in my arms lost in the wilds of Argentina.

What is our book? A search for the right form. A few words, a few images. And one or two secrets.

The secret of the piece of paper the colonel holds in his right hand as he kneels on the grass, his left hand clutching his face.

The secret of Sarah's death.

The secret of who knows. It's a bit like a Persian tale: it takes a lifetime to write and a hundred to read. And only one to forget. But no, it takes two lives to write. And if we lack innocence, let me write these pages that a child can read.

One night I woke up screaming. I saw Sarah's death in a dream. And my scream became lost in time, until today, until these words which I never wanted.

Sarah and I had developed a taste for a certain type of freedom. We liked being outsiders.

After Fontainebleau, we returned to Stanmore and our house: Westwood. The garden gave onto the 'green belt'. The thatched roof gave it an old-fashioned feel. Westwood had a fairytale charm and a soul.

Sarah started at the French Lycée. She would disappear every morning into the London Underground on her way to South Kensington. On a secret adventure.

Sarah stayed with the French, while I went back to uniform and discipline. It was painful, this return to barracks.

Mathematics resisted my every attempt to grasp them. I discovered that numbers literally stopped me in my tracks. I had terrible turns at school, like fainting fits. I'd fall over. Was it because I didn't understand? Was it some logical terror?

The school and my father were consulted. I was dispensed from maths lessons. And that is how a part of the world remains a mystery to me ever since, paralysing and fascinating me in equal measure.

Stop the world. I want to get off. Everyone can keep going but I have to stop.

What do you think if I stay where I am for hours and days and weeks on end. The outside world barred. All dialogue shot. Your words are snares, you know that very well … Nausea without definition. All illusions gone.

We create our universe in the attic. Our own world: a big sitting-room, two bedrooms. Sarah and I bring up armchairs and books. This is our poetic horizon.

On Sunday afternoons we invite people over. My mother, who has always loved balls, parties, dressing up, enthusiastically encourages us. 'Charlotte and Sarah's parties' become a thing locally.

Our friends sit quietly on chairs, on the floor: we drink orange juice, listen to records, sing and dance, rock'n'roll and slows.

Listening and singing. The 45s fall on the spindle of the record-player.

Sarah and I often speak French, our secret language. Everything seems innocent. It is an open-ended, happy time. Our golden age.

When love steps in and takes you for a spin,
oh là là là c'est magnifique
and when one night
your loved one holds you tight
oh là là là c'est magnifique
but when one day
your loved one drifts away
oh là là là it is so tragique
but when once more
he whispers je t'adore
c'est magnifique …

The music fills us, lulls us into a gentle reverie, and in a sense, speaks for us as well.

The atmosphere in Stanmore's parish hall at the start of that summer was hard to believe. The room was packed. I remember the sound of rustling, of laughter.

Sarah and I were in raincoats and fishnets. We wore berets. We sang Luis Mariano, our versions. It was *so French* …

Afterwards people came up to me. They seemed surprised: 'Charlotte, we didn't know you had it in you!'

I started to see. To understand a certain way of looking at people that wins them over. Holds them, challenges them. The look that disappears when you leave the stage.

I was fourteen and I've never forgotten that unsettling, thrilling feeling.

And then you felt people were staring at your face, your grey eyes, heavy-lidded and distant, your body, your smile, your grace.

Years later, when my father and I started talking, he said in all earnestness, 'If I had to start over, I'd be an actor.'

In Stanmore, he played the lead in Terence Rattigan's play, *The Deep Blue Sea*. Liberated from the army, from its uniforms and traditions, he metamorphosed into a clumsy, eccentric leading man. I was amazed to see him walk out on stage, suddenly so free. This is the English spirit: they admire eccentricity. The joy has got to express itself somehow.

I saw my mother dancing in fishnet stockings in front of the whole town, including her daughters and her husband, and she was happy.

After a concert in Stanmore, an agent sought out Sarah and me and offered us an audition at a club in Piccadilly.

We made plans for this expedition, which had to be kept secret. What would our parents think of us sneaking up to London like that?

We hid our berets and raincoats in our satchels. Then one afternoon we rushed off after school. A mad scramble on the Underground, then through the streets of Piccadilly ... I can still feel our feverish elation.

We sang in front of three gloomy men who didn't say a thing. Melancholy hung in the air. I can still see the look in their eyes as they watched us across the empty tables.

Then the Underground swallowed us up again: we didn't say a word until we got home. The colonel was waiting for us on the steps. He stared at Sarah and me in silence, as if he knew. And that was the end of my career as a cabaret singer.

Even childhood with its vague and happy memories, the songs, the beaches, the waiting; neatly folded hands; laughter; lost images; the going away and coming back – all this can make a book too.

Aren't you writing any more?
I don't know.
Each day disappears when another one starts.
As if we no longer need the eternal round of gestures and rituals, the to and fro of a day. So I forget and disappear only to begin again.

One day, it's not the day. The door of the fifth floor is half-open. I cross the room. It's strange, it's as though this scene has already happened. Sitting at your desk, you are staring at the screen. A long text is scrolling down in front of you.

We have tea.

You call London. And those pages that were making you cry have disappeared.

Little, so little, so wild that I am. Silent witness of uncontrolled minds. Silence becomes a voice without words. Irresistible urge of violence contained. Impulses that collide and knock me off course. Scattered through my story as markers of my way.

I'm back. I'm not quite sure where at the moment.

Sarah is sensual and defenceless somehow, I'm not sure really how to explain it. She has an uncommon grace and innocence. On that day I am playing big sister, that's the part I've been given. I am her bodyguard, her protector.

Sarah is sixteen and I am just fourteen. We are wearing light, summery dresses. Tom, her boyfriend, is on his own in the front of his tiny three-wheeler bubble car. I am sitting on Sarah's lap in the back. We are racing through the countryside on our way to Oxford.

The bubble car is going down a long hill at top speed when a construction truck slowly pulls out without seeing us. Tom brakes like mad. We are going far too fast. We are far too heavy. Death is inevitable.

Miraculously, our bubble car got past. We drove another hundred yards, then Tom pulled over to the side, trembling, white as a sheet. We sat on the grass in the sun. I'll never forget the sensation, *the feeling of being alive*.

Later, on that same summer day, Sarah and Tom slipped away, their arms around each other's waists. They walked off and lay down in the grass. I sat patiently waiting. I was just there. I was probably hoping for some whispering, rustling. Then Tom emerged into the sunlight, followed by Sarah. Scrutinising her beautiful face, I saw she was different, excited, miles away. I sensed a mystery in her.

Sometimes I wish that all of life could be contained in my gaze.

What cannot be said must be dreamed. When you dream, you cherish your secret.

My father had a bubble car too: an eccentric amalgam of metal and plastic with three wheels and no door. To get in you lifted up the see-through bubble and climbed in over the handlebars. Colonel Rampling was a sight to behold driving through Stanmore in his uniform, upright and concentrated. People would turn and stare as he passed, but he took no notice.

Later, I found out the make of Tom's bubble car that nearly killed the three of us on that day of sunshine and pleasure: it was a Kabinenroller. Because they had worked for the Reich, Messerschmitt were forbidden to produce aircraft after the war, so their factories recycled planes into these strange vehicles ... Then the bubble cars disappeared – along with transparency, the colonel, certain memories, playfulness, the aircraft factories – and then cars all looked the same.

London was dancing. The Blitz was a thing of the past. No more tears and deprivation. We were alive.

Everything was different: skirts, music, objects, language, freedom, the riot of colour on every wall, friends, bars and restaurants, the visible and invisible. We were the baby boomers. All the codes were turned on their heads. There was a rhythm, a mutation, a collective heartbeat.

A historic, indefinable moment.

And soon we would never be the same again.

I'll keep silent about the things that are not in these pages. Other people will talk.

And they don't know. They poke around and repeat what others have said. Who wouldn't want to walk joyously down the King's Road in a miniskirt in the 60s? Who wouldn't want to devote their life to the movies? To photographers? I was, and I still am, that woman.

Eventually I opened the diaries my mother kept as a young girl, with her writings in purple ink, pale shades of violet and coloured pencils. I discovered events and thoughts detailed in her careful handwriting. My mother was a romantic. She made lists of the boys she liked, as though she was learning how to fall in love. Some were good dancers. Others were fun, distant. Charming, dashing or dreadful. My mother was dreamy and had many suitors. At one point someone called Godgers appears in the lists – her affectionate nickname for my father. Gradually the lists stop, and the diaries with them, as if they had been suspended in time until they landed in my hands.

to me as I really like
I just cant bare to
think that my Godges is
going away tomorrow. today
He has been so sweet
he gave my hand he
most lovely kiss which
I can feel to this
minute he is such an
absolute darly I am
complelly head over heels
in love with him Darly
Godges I just longed
for him to kiss me tonight
but sometimes, when he
is teerd he seems almost
inhuman I know he
doesnt mean to hurt
my feelings because he
has got a sweet nature

I found out the truth about Sarah three years after her death.

She took her secret away with her when she took away her life.

She killed herself on 14 February 1967, after having given birth prematurely to a baby boy on 13 January in a hospital in Buenos Aires.

When I asked my father why he had kept such a secret, he said, 'It would kill your mother if she knew.'

So this became our secret and I've always wondered if Mum was protected by our pact or poisoned by the lie.

Perhaps this is it, the cutting edge of truth: a secret that keeps us human.

My mother and I stand in front of the mirror. We contemplate our images. Her reflection mirrors a woman she no longer recognises. Her eyes follow the trail of my sister. Her mouth speaks but I cannot hear. Silence settles between us.

My father stands before me. He says I am young. He says I must go out into the world and not look back. He says he will always be there for my mother. He says, 'Charlotte, you don't have to come back for us'.

I am standing at the window of a hotel in a country whose language and customs are strange to me. I am a stranger.

I am in a city that I do not know and that does not know me.

I observe from afar the daily ritual of everyday lives. The distance is reassuring. The hidden side of life shows a truth that transparency conceals.

Everything is still, nothing moves. The city drowses in the scorching heat. I wait by my window for the movement to begin again. Waiting is anything but passive. Waiting is listening. Waiting is about knowing when to move on.

I am immobile. I am weary. I wait for time to pass. I am haunted by the passage of time.

I have come here to forget who I am. To find other images to erase those that hide the truth.

I want to listen to a language with unfamiliar sounds. I want to perform rituals without knowing from whence they came. I am seeking a silent encounter to find the right words.

My sister died a violent death.

I saw my family sink into silence.

I took flight and became a stranger among strangers. An unconscious quest guided me here.

I spent a long time in the wilderness before I could shed my first tear and be relieved of the pain so long denied.

The colonel died peacefully in his sleep.

He had just turned a hundred and he joined my mother who had died ten years earlier.

At the end his skin was grey, his pulse slow. I didn't go back to see him, without really knowing why. There's still always time, isn't there?

A few prayers, a little music, two readings, the family. Absolute simplicity, just as he would have wanted.

The words have come. After how many years? A walk in the wilderness. It's this very book.

One night I get a message from the end of the world: *I'm sitting beside Sarah.*

I shiver.

My son is writing to me from Buenos Aires. He is with Sarah's son. They barely know one another.

Charlotte's son and Sarah's son.

David and Carlos Jr.

They are young men now.

They walk along the main avenue of the cemetery like laughing children.

They go to your grave together.

They stay with you.

It seems that I can finally see that distant landscape, feel the southern heat, touch the grieving earth, watch the tall trees bending over you. It seems that I am getting close to you.

It seems that these words were not the hard road but a poem that was reaching out for you.

Sarah, you seem to be here: in this book, in these years, in this childhood, our childhood.

Sarah, you seem gentle, absent, joyful, and unforgettable, and those two young men, sitting on your grave in silence, have brought my poem to an end.

Charlotte Rampling is an acclaimed English actor with a stellar career in international films across three languages, known for films such as *45 Years* (for which she received an Oscar nomination), *Swimming Pool*, and *The Night Porter*. She lives in France.

Christophe Bataille is a novelist and publisher, and the author, with Rithy Panh, of *Elimination* (Grasset, 2012) which won the Elle Grand Readers' Prize.

William Hobson's translations include Alexandre Dumas' *The Three Musketeers* and Samir Kassir's *Being Arab*, winner of the Index on Censorship Freedom of Expression Award.